Diane Von Furstenberg

$37.50 US

THE BATH

THE BATH

DIANE VON FURSTENBERG

Photographs by
STEWART O'SHIELDS

Design by
LIZ TROVATO

Produced by
OLIVIER GELBSMANN

 RANDOM HOUSE, NEW YORK

Manufactured in Italy
24689753
First Edition

Library of Congress Cataloging-in-Publication Data
Von Furstenberg, Diane.
The bath / by Diane Von Furstenberg : photographs by Stewart O'Shields.
p.   cm.
ISBN 0-679-42679-5
1. Bathing customs—History.
GT2845.V66   1993
391'.64'09—dc20   93-3626

To my brother, Philippe

ACKNOWLEDGMENTS

The Bath is the continuation of the exhilarating journey I began with *Beds*. We continued our travels to Hungary, Italy, France, England, and many towns and cities throughout the United States, encountering old friends, and making new ones.

Asking permission to enter a private oasis of cleanliness, intimacy, and beauty is a delicate matter. But the responses to our calls and letters were overwhelmingly gracious and kind. My deepest thanks to all those who opened their homes to us and to our cameras—including those who, for lack of space, could not be included in the finished book. It is my hope that this collection of photographs reflects our respect and enthusiasm for the rooms we photographed.

I wish to thank so many people for making *The Bath* a reality. First, my friend Olivier Gelbsmann, without whose flawless style, creativity, and global coordination this work would never have been possible. I have been able to entrust him with everything from organizing photo shoots on an international scale to tracking down minute historical details to help me realize this book.

Stewart O'Shields's extraordinary talents and endless energy translated our international journey into a magnificent photographic tour. Many sincere thanks as well to Antoine Meyer, David Seidner, Gwendoline Ffoulke, Cynthia Oliviera Cezar, Cookie Kinkead, Ozan Gulek, Ivan Terestchenko, Loic Raout, and Erica Lennard for their superb photographic contributions.

My sincere gratitude to Susan Bell for her astute guidance, to Katherine Rosenbloom and Gail Blackhall at Random House for their great assistance, to Liz Trovato for her artistic talent, to Geoffrey Freitag and Nancy Rabinowitz for their eloquence, to Mary Tantillo, Janet Kanzia, Lisa Gabbay, and Simona Passalacqua for their coordination, and to the many friends, artists, decorators, architects, curators, and writers who helped us so generously to make this possible:

Eugene Braun-Munk

Colonel de Roquemaurel

Nicole Altero

Dr. Bhandari

J.P. Beaujard

Minnie de Beauvau Craon

Sig Bergamin

Marie Claire Blancaert

Ronald Bricke

Milly and Roger de Cabrol

Stephanie Cauchoix

François Catroux

Gilles de Chabaneix

Gloria Cohen

Madison Cox

Paul Durkes

Marilyn Evins

Nicolle Fallot

Sue Feinberg

Egon Von Furstenberg

Christoph Gollut

Barry Goralnick

Christiane Graziani

Romain Graziani

Geraldine Grinda

Gerald N. Jacobs

Konstantine Kakanias

Kenzo

David Kleinberg

Dorothy Ko

Richard Keith Langham

Peter Marino

Juan Montoya

Richard Perry

Christopher Petnakas and Ami Li

Françoise de Pfyffer

Alberto Pinto

Andrée Putman

Craig Raywood

Michael La Rocca

Daniel Romualdez

Bruno Roy

Guillaume Saalburg

Michael de Santis

Claudia and Ed Sirakowit

Alana Stewart

Mitchell Strohl

Elisabeth Mary Stuart

Nona Summers

Ali Tayer

Julian Tomchin

Pilar Vilaris

Peter Vitale

Natalie Zimmerman

Let me say thank you to the following people for respecting our vision, and welcoming us into their homes to photograph their private sanctuary, the bathroom:

Paul and Lucy Audouy

Jacques Badois

Fabio Belloti

Nora Bentick

Pierre Berge

Marisa Berenson

Mark Birley

Mr. and Mrs. Masakasu Bokura

Murielle Brandolini

Cecille Chancelle

Richard Cohen

Barry Diller

Rudi Dordoni

Luigi D'Urso and Ines de la
    Fressange

Lisa Eisner

Romana Fabris

Donatella Flick

Angelica Frescobaldi

Sandy Gallin

Larry Gagosian

Isabel Goldsmith

Didier Grumbach

Lynda Guber

Susan Harris

Ralph Harvard

Jed Johnson

Nancy Jerry Kitch

Kelly and Calvin Klein

Marc Landeau

Pierre and Marianne de Malleray
    de Barre

Sue Mengers

Sally Metcalf

Jane Millet

Joachim Molina

Daniela Morera

Mrs. Nataf

Mr. and Mrs. Carlos Pagani

Mr. and Mrs. Patrikoff

Johnny Pigozzi

Alberto Pinto

Giordano Restelli

Martin Richards

Nile Rodgers

Beatrice de Rothschild

Eliane Scali

Ian Schrager

Joel Silver

Ane Summers

Mrs. Tapiau

Rose Tarlow

Jean Claude Tramont

Patsy Tish

Nicholas Garcia Uriburu

Gianni Versace

Alan Wazenberg

And many thanks to:

HUNGARY

Direction of Municipal Bath of
    Budapest—Hedwig Molnar,
    Esaba Mesko

Gellert Medicinal Bath, Budapest

Szechenyi Therapeutic Bath,
    Budapest

Kiraly Thermal Bath, Budapest

USA

Hot Springs , Arkansas

Greenbrier Hot Spring,
    West Virginia

Saratoga Hot Spring, New York

The Royalton, New York

Golden Door Spa, California—
    Robin Cruise

Morgans, New York—
    Anda Andrei

The Bel-Air, California

In Asheville, North Carolina, water gushes out of a bronze lion's head into a sunken recessed Roman-style bath.

Villa Vizcaya Museum,
    Florida—Doris Littlefield

Biltmore Estate,
    North Carolina—Julia Weede

The Image Bank, New York

Pratesi Linen, New York

Floris Perfumes, New York

Puiforcat Silverware, New York

FRANCE

Evian Thermal Bath

Vichy Thermal Bath

Royal Monceau, Paris—
    Claudine Cadoret

Villa Kerylos, Beaulieu—
    Institute of France

Atelier d'Images, Paris—
    Brigitte Richon

Epi d'Or bath accessories, Paris

Musée de l'école de Nancy—
    Georges Barbier Ludwig

ITALY

Terme Berziere, Salsomaggiore

Grand Hotel La Pace—
    Claudio Tongiorgi

Palace of Caserta—
    Professor Iacobitti

Tawaraya in Kyoto, Japan

The Claridges, London

C O N T

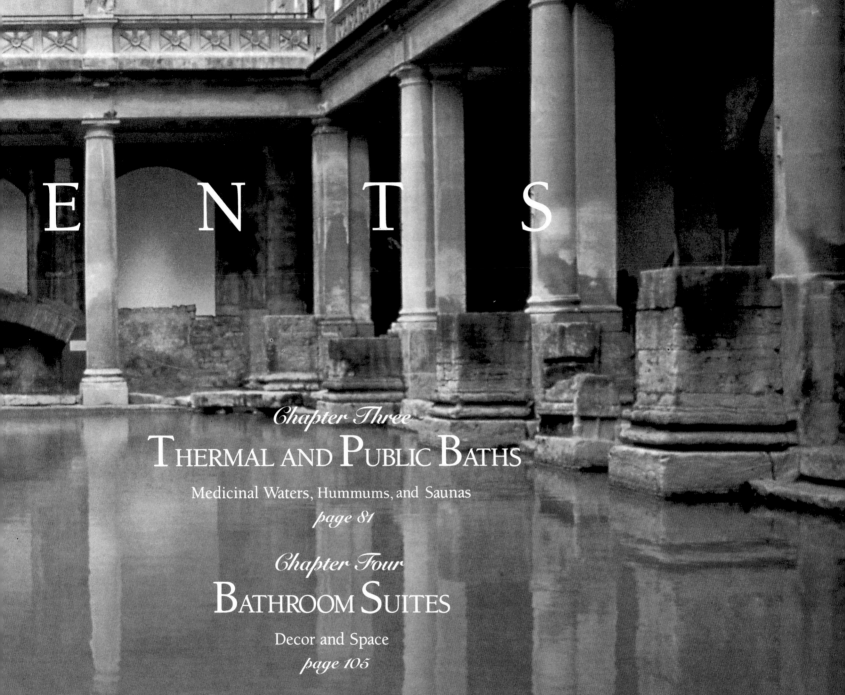

INTRODUCTION

The bath is the cradle for communion with life, because water is the source of all that lives. Through the ritual of bathing we worship water. The sanctity of the bath heals, while its privacy soothes, creating a precious refuge from daily stress. One bathes for cleanliness and purification, but also for serenity, isolation, and pleasure.

The bath has existed since antiquity, as documented by the Egyptians, Greeks, and Persians. Ever since the scented atmosphere of Roman baths married the dual concerns of hygiene and enjoyment, the therapeutic properties of water have remained a constant source of renewal to our health and beauty.

The first bath takes place at the moment of birth, after the baby is separated from the mother's body. From that day forward, the child experiences the daily ritual of bathing, which divides day from night, activity from calm; so begins his lifelong relationship with water. The bath will become, as the child grows up, a habit, a necessity, a luxury, a private moment of peace and pleasure.

Water is miracle, reward, and punishment, as the legend of Noah reminds us. In the Christian religion, baptism is received through ablution. In most faiths, bathing precedes important religious ceremonies, often playing a part in fertility rituals.

Public bathhouses have always been gathering places where people come in search of relaxation and water's medicinal effects. Whole towns with luxury hotels and spas have been created around beneficial natural springs, whose waters have been bottled and marketed.

In modern times, bathrooms have become sanctuaries for architectural and decorative beauty. Some are hi-tech, with sauna, hot tub, and exercise equipment, while others resemble drawing rooms, where personal beauty paraphernalia, like body oils, soaps, and loofahs, mix with fine art, books, and photographs. Showers are popular for their speed and efficiency, but baths remain the rite passed down from our ancestors, who understood the need for hygiene and pleasure.

This book is meant to be a visual journey through the history of the bath and an inspirational overview of its aesthetics.

Diane Von Furstenberg

The Source of the Bath

*P*urifying and quenching, rejuvenating and soothing, water channels through every day of our lives. From the Garden of Eden, bountiful waters issued forth, flowing out from the center of Paradise to give birth to all of life in its many forms. Coursing across the crust of the earth, these waters formed a brilliant blue web, filling vast seas and delicate ponds, frothing rivers and spectacular waterfalls. Here, a unique environment was created: quiet, protective . . . the ideal setting for the first living organisms to take form.

The Mesopotamians, whose culture emerged at the edges of the Tigris and Euphrates rivers, were the first to master water, changing the course of its powerful flow to suit their own purposes. Excavations in the enormous Mesopotamian Palace of Mari, buried under centuries of dust and soil, have revealed some of the earliest evidence of bathrooms, dating back to the eighteenth century B.C. In one of these bathrooms was a double tub constructed of clay, perhaps designed to allow a king and a queen to bathe simultaneously, or a single bather to enjoy the contrast of hot and cold water.

On the banks of the Nile, the Egyptian civilization took root. By the sixteenth century B.C., bathing had a place at the center of certain religious activities. Four times a day, priests were required to chill their bodies in cold water. Some rituals required them to shave from head to toe

Detail of a young woman washing her hair, Greece, fourth century B.C. Provincial museum of Lecce.

Blue dolphin fresco, Knossos, Greece. Photo by Antonio Bignami, IMG.

Reconstitution of the antique baths of Caracalla in Rome. Bibliothèque Art Décoratif, Paris, above. *Portico at the baths,* left.

before performing their daily duties for the gods. For the Egyptians, external beauty and appearance were extremely important. As in modern culture, entire rooms were devoted to the bathing ritual, which was traditionally followed by massage and, finally, anointment with exotic scents.

Hygiene and cleanliness became central to the Mosaic law of the Hebrews when Moses, inspired by God, prescribed ablutions to his people. One was to bathe following contact with impurity, the ill, or the dead; women were to bathe during the seven days of their monthly cycle. Following the bath, prayer heightened the purification of body and soul. In some religions, bathing before daily prayers and religious celebrations is still practiced today.

On the Greek island of Crete lie fragments of once-magnificent Minoan sanctuaries and palaces: Phaistos, Zakro, Knossos. Through stone and glazed pottery pipes, the Minoans brought fresh running water from the rivers into the city reservoirs of Knossos. The sophisticated irrigation system provided water for kitchens, baths, and ceremonial pools. At Knossos, palace walls reflect this civilization's praise for water: in the queen's quarters, a beautiful fresco depicts an aquatic scene of dolphins leaping out of the sea.

The Greeks showed a marked preference for cold baths, enjoying the fresh, cool-flowing rivers and springs as well as sea bathing. Among those of a stoic sensibility, the hot bath was believed to induce indolence and to weaken the body; but it was occa-

sionally permitted as a special in-dulgence for those who had earned a reward. Homer describes the mythic characters Ulysses and Diomedes each washing off the sweat of battle in the turbulent sea before retreating to the calm, contained waters of the bath. In the Grecian manner, water was warmed in a bronze cauldron that rested on a pedestal over the fire. Women were charged with tending to the ablutions, pouring water out of the cauldron onto the bathers. Even Helen and Circe are said to have attended warriors at their bath. After cleansing, the bathers were surrounded with the scents of fragrant oils and precious perfumes. Thus were they prepared for their dinner, which in Greek tradition was nearly always preceded by bathing.

Through writings and works of art, the bathing rituals of everyday Greek life come vividly alive. Painted onto the pottery of the ancient Greeks are scenes of the most common form of bathing, the cold shower, popularized in the fourth century B.C. after

Fresco "Della Venere nella Conchiglia," Pompeii, above. Palestra, the courtyard at the Stabiae Baths, Pompeii, right.

Decorative washbasin surmounted by lion's head, symbolic of the antique Greek style, Kerylos, above.

Men's Caldarium, at the Stabiae Baths, Pompeii, left.

Pisistratus installed appropriate public facilities. In fountains and palaestrae throughout Athens, waters arched in the brilliant sunlight. Men and women bathed nude at the public baths and porticoes, showering in water that spouted from the mouths of animal heads, sculpted in stone. These extraordinary creatures, modeled after wild boars and panthers, symbolized the imaginary sources of the water itself.

Today, it is possible to experience a remarkable re-creation of the Greek life-style at Villa Kerylos, constructed from 1902 to 1908 in the South of France by Theodore Reinach and Emmanuel Pontremoli, and now accessible as a museum. The elegant architecture of classic antiquity has been a source of inspiration throughout the ages; nowhere in the world, not even in Greece, does there exist a more accurate replica of it than at Kerylos. Standing amidst the noble purity of the cut stone and marble, overlooking the blue Mediterranean Sea, one can sense how Ulysses must have enjoyed such decor.

Surely the art of the bath reached its grandest, most elegant expression under the Roman Empire. Bathing was a principal form of social interaction and recreation for the Romans. Attended by virtually all on a daily basis, the baths were a place to enjoy swimming and other exercise, exotic health treatments, the latest gossip, and sumptuous meals. The day's visit might include diversions ranging from therapeutic massages to lectures on philosophy and art. Propriety, however, gave way to decadence and excess as the empire's fall approached. Caligula is said to have gratified his whims by swallowing pearls dissolved in aromatic vinegar while soaking in scented oils, and Heliogabalus allegedly took on the task of bathing with all the prostitutes of Rome. Banquets and orgies became so commonly associated with the baths that the emperor Adrian banned mixed-sex bathing, limiting the sensual indulgence in the bathhouse.

Satisfying the boundless thirst of Rome's many baths in their

Gilt silver lion-head faucets with seashell soap holder, Kerylos.

heyday required plentiful water from streams and, most important, the river Tiber. Aqueducts were the ingenious Roman solution to carrying water from its natural source into the city's brilliantly designed fountains, pools, and the public baths. These baths sometimes offered the luxury of constantly flowing hot springs.

Thermal baths were a hallmark of Roman civilization, erected not only in Italy, but throughout the vast empire as it stretched across Europe. These baths were of immense proportions and were surrounded by spacious, beautiful

Greek Revival bathroom at Villa Kerylos, Beaulieu, France. The monolithic bath standing on lion-paw feet is carved in white marble.

grounds. Bathing facilities consisted of courtyards and porticoes: typically, each offered a variety of environments to experience. From the apodyterium, a vestibule for undressing, the bather could move on to the piscina, or swimming pool; or to the calderium or sudarium, the steam bath or sauna, to induce a cleansing, calming sweat; the frigidarium, an invigorating cold-water pool; the balneum, for a warm-water bath; and the tepidarium, a place to rest.

The bather arriving at Caracalla in Rome crossed the threshold into a dramatic interior space. Spectacular, high ceilings were surmounted by cupolas, and inlaid marble, mosaics, and porphyry lined the walls. From faucets of gold and silver, the waters gushed out to as many as twenty-five hundred bathers at a time. The citizens, dwarfed by majestic columns, could move through the facility's network of corridors, passing in and out of galleries, lecture halls, massage rooms, and shops for as long as they desired.

Pompeii's thermal baths at Stabiae were known as the baths at the heart of a park, because of the lavish greenery that surrounded them. Here, nature made the retreat to the bath in itself a delight to the senses. Bathers could wander along walkways, surrounded by the sounds of flowing fountains and the scents of cypresses, olive trees, palm trees, gardenia bushes, roses, and other fragrant flowers. In the Roman tradition, bathing transported the bather to a more idyllic realm.

From the perfumed atmosphere of the Roman baths emerged a style of bathing that truly married the concerns of hygiene and pleasure, health care and luxury, and demonstrated a respect for sensual pleasure in settings of great beauty. The Romans were among the first to unlock the remarkable therapeutic qualities of the bath. They found in water's purity both spiritual and aesthetic inspiration, celebrating it as a central focus of everyday life.

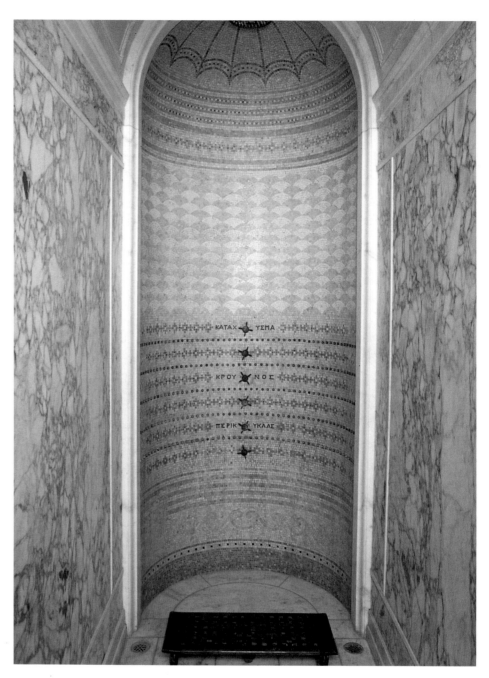

Inlaid mosaic shower, Villa Kerylos, above.

Sunken octagonal marble bath in the Greco-Roman classical style, Kerylos, right.

At the Villa Kerylos, France : a pair of cast silver porpoise taps crowned by swans, above. Classical antique bath, right. Ivory-inlaid wooden vanity flanked by a pair of bronze washbasins in classical antique style, left.

At the Milan home of Gianni Versace, the
elliptic bath area is designed in a style
reminiscent of the ancient Roman tradition,
above and right.

Private Baths

W hen we draw closed the door to the bathroom, we seal ourselves off from the outside world. For a brief while, we are in a world of our own.

Until just one century ago, this luxury of privacy was largely unknown in all but the wealthiest homes. Although bathtubs of many sizes and shapes, made of wood, stone, marble, zinc, iron, or even silver, have been in use since antiquity, the fully functioning

At the Castle of La Roche Courbon in France, a bath in an alcove was added to a magnificent seventeenth-century salon of paintings, above.

Outside view of the castle of La Roche Courbon, built in 1475 by Jehan de La Tour and restored to pristine condition by Jacques and Marie-Jeanne Badois, left.

A period bath at the Castle of Valencay, 1830.

bathroom in the home, with toilet, tub, sink, and running water, remained an uncommon privilege throughout most of history.

The habit of bathing has varied greatly over the centuries. During the Middle Ages, the focus of bathing was not hygiene so much as the indulgence of physical pleasures. The common people visited the public baths for feasting, drinking, and erotic pursuits; the very rich took part in the same activities at home. The private bathtub was a place to entertain guests and flaunt one's wealth. In round, vat-shaped tubs made of wood and lined with linen, the bathers would soak under a draped canopy, listening to musical entertainment and being served an ostentatious assortment of expensive food and drink by their host. Not surprisingly, this was the scene for many an elaborate seduction. Such indulgences became so commonly associated with the bath that a religious backlash finally denounced bathing altogether.

By the sixteenth century, esca-

lating health concerns provided support for this tide of moral disfavor. The plagues and other widespread diseases of the Middle Ages had inspired a growing belief that water itself was a carrier of infections. Most people went to great lengths to avoid water, having been warned that exposure to it would open the pores and weaken the constitution.

Bathing thus became a matter more of etiquette than of hygiene, the object being to maintain the appearance of cleanliness by keeping clean what was visible to others. Hands and face were washed, and clothing was frequently changed: King Louis XIV is said to have had innumerable clean white linen shirts at the ready for his frequent daily changes. But with respect to the rest of the body, "cleaning" mostly meant masking odors. Perfumes and powders were heavily applied, and rubbing, often with the likes of rose petals and other freshening agents, was widely practiced. Scent boxes were everywhere; cinnamon water was a popular means of disguising

Placed on a slab of marble, porcelain set stamped with the gold insignia of Mrs. Vanderbilt harkens back to an earlier time when bowls and pitchers were used in lieu of sinks for daily cleansing, top.

Mr. George Washington Vanderbilt's lion-footed tub, carved in marble, employed a complex water-heating mechanism that regulated water temperature even more consistently than contemporary systems, above.

At the Biltmore Estate in Asheville, North Carolina, Mrs. Vanderbilt's porcelain tub standing on lion-paws features an elaborate shower, a rare luxury in 1895, right.

bad breath. To clean the hair, moisture-absorbing powders were applied at bedtime and combed out in the morning. If at all possible, water did not enter the routine.

As was typical of this era, the Palace of Versailles was erected entirely without plumbing. Though six bathrooms were installed during his reign, Louis XIV is said to have bathed only twice in his life and to have taken terribly ill after each occasion. The king is more commonly associated with the 264 *chaises percées* he is said to have installed. This modified chamber pot, incorporating a chair with a hole in the seat, was often manufactured of precious materials, some painted with landscapes and upholstered with velour.

The flush toilet, though a rarity, was not unknown before modern times. It was invented for Queen Elizabeth in 1596 by her godson, Sir John Harrington. Unfortunately, the device fell into obscurity until a British mathematician and watchmaker, Alexander Cumming, updated Har-

A guest washroom with a decorative sink carved from a wooden block, Bel Air.

Chaise percée in a Renaissance style, Bel Air, California.

rington's design in 1775, adding a water barrier to block the passage of odors from the cesspool. Despite this advance, it was not until the end of the nineteenth century that the invention began to appear in British homes.

For the most part, even at the end of the eighteenth century, running water was available only in a select few aristocratic homes, and cleanliness was considered a luxury, rather than a necessity, as it is today. Slowly, however, bathing regained popularity: 150 baths existed in Paris in 1790; ten years later, the number had doubled. And among sixty-six mansions in the area in 1801, twenty-one featured private bathrooms.

Balzac, in an 1837 letter, reflects the ambivalence that greeted the growing claims of the medical establishment that bathing was beneficial. The author queasily describes his feelings that a bath would be advantageous to his health, but might well weaken his constitution and strike down his productivity indefinitely.

Others were more progressive.

Rose Tarlow brings the charm of the past into the present, Bel Air, California.

Benjamin Franklin brought the first bathtub to the United States in the 1780s. He is said to have passed many hours in the tub writing as he soaked. In 1810, the first three-piece bathroom with toilet, tub, and washbasin appeared in Philadelphia, a city that had some of the best plumbing yet built. But in 1851, when President Millard Fillmore had a bathtub installed in the White House, he was criticized for indulging in "monarchical luxury."

The value of a daily bathing regimen received powerful reinforcement in the public mind in 1870, when Louis Pasteur's discoveries confirmed the existence of a hidden bacterial world. But an even greater influence in repopularizing bathing hygiene had begun earlier in the nineteenth century with the "back to nature" movement. It was inspired by Rousseau and a Swiss naturalist and "healer," Pressneitz. Pressneitz developed a complete program of outdoor exercise, which included showers taken outside in water channeled from nearby springs.

At the Paris home of Marisa Berenson, sheer white draperies add an air of mystery to a romantic palette, left. *Photo by Antoine Meyer.*

François Catroux maximized the tall proportions of a small room to create a look that radiates casual elegance, above. *Diane Von Furstenberg bath, Paris, France, 1992.*

By the middle of the nine-teenth century, running water be-gan to work its way into everyday life. Citywide plumbing systems channeled water directly into the home, at first only to the base-ment, from which buckets would be carted to other parts of the house. Slowly, technology took advantage of water pressure, and at last, running-water taps could exist wherever they were desired. It was the end of an age of water carriers, like little Cosette of Hugo's *Les Misérables*, who earned a meager sum by hauling pails of water from city fountains to pri-vate homes.

Around the turn of the century during La Belle Époque, a rather clear change in bathing patterns appeared. The Industrial Rev-olution reduced manufacturing costs, while also creating greater affluence in the general popula-tion. Now, more people could af-ford the luxuries being intro-duced by manufacturers.

Among these was the bathtub. With the advent of the modern age, hot running water, and sewer systems, the tub finally stabi-

For a Paris townhouse, artist and sculptor Mario de Gultz brilliantly realized with glass and mirrors a bathroom that reflects translucence and lightness, left. Peter Valentiner used military camouflage fabric to create a decorative curtain, right.

43

lized: no longer portable, it came off its legs and took a recessed position in the bathroom. A basic trilogy emerged as the primary components of this room: the bathtub, sink, and toilet, and, later, the bidet. A different lifestyle radically changed everyday life. At last after so many centuries, the private bathroom in every home became a reality.

At the Vanderbilt mansion in Asheville, North Carolina, Mrs. Vanderbilt's bathroom was installed with a porcelain tub and a state-of-the-art shower, but was curiously missing a running-water sink. Instead, an exquisite porcelain washbowl and pitcher with the family insignia stamped in gold still remain on a slab of marble. This bathroom is very evocative of the turn of the century, when past customs lived together with modern technology.

As the American bathroom evolved, the American hotel became a significant trendsetter. The Mount Vernon Hotel in Cape May, New Jersey, created a sensation when it opened in 1853—it

had running water in each of its rooms. Few could match this standard until 1908, when a Buffalo hotel made news with the slogan "A Room and a Bath for a Dollar and a Half." In American homes, too, the bathroom adjacent to the bedroom would become a regular feature. Hotels also influenced the American bathroom through their economy of scale. Emphasizing compactness and purity of form, the

Design by architect John Wolfe. Pink marble was chosen to suit the sunken bath at Mr. and Mrs. Jean Claude Tramont's home in Beverly Hills, California, above.

In an alcove, a sunken black marble tub sets the tone for an Art Deco room in the Paris pied-à-terre of Eliane Scali, right.

Period prints and muted tones create a romantic setting at the home of Mr. and Mrs.
Pierre de Malleray de Barre at Maison
Lafitte near Paris, above. Antique sink
reminiscent of the turn of the century, right.

hotel-style bathroom eventually won out over a more English inclination toward large-scale bathrooms with furniture-like components.

The standardization of the bathroom proceeded with the introduction of the mass-produced tub. The five-foot-long recessed tub quickly became the norm, and bathrooms were designed around its dimensions. Soon, the bathroom was a consistent presence in every home, a room of few surprises.

The modern bathroom encourages the hypnotic patterns of daily personal routines, performed without words, with barely a thought. It is natural that we should readily believe this to be a room that has always existed. Today, we simply turn a knob and the rumbling water fills the room with its steamy vapors. We undress, test the temperature, and step in, slowly adjusting to the penetrating heat. We are free to disappear into the deep, serene comfort of privacy.

In London, Ane Summers brought the bath into the bedroom to create warmth and intimacy, above.

English-style bath by Sally Metcalf, London, left.

In a Manhattan penthouse, artist Jane Millet designed a distinctive medieval-style bath for a gentleman, right.

With a discriminating taste for American arts and crafts, Jed Johnson and Alan Wanzenberg chose the lustrous and richly colored "Pewabic" ceramic tiles, expressing a contained elegance for this New York bathroom, left.

In a Manhattan townhouse the bathroom has been stylized with antiques brought back from far-away countries by an avid art collector. The antique brass shower was found at a Portobello flea market in London. The washbasin has been set into a pinewood cabinet found in an English barbershop and the Turkish lanterns were brought back from Istanbul, right.

In a California villa ample space has been
given to the bath. An oval marble tub stands
in front of a curved wall made of glass bricks,
to maximize daylight, above.

The Hampton bath of art collector Larry
Gagosian, designed by architect Charles
Gwathmey, right.

Nineteen-fifties-style bath in Milan, top.

With great style, Milanese antiquarian An-
gelica Frescobaldi cleverly used every square
inch of her loft to install a charming bath
area, above.

In Milan, architect Rudi Dordoni chose
muted earth tones for his bath.

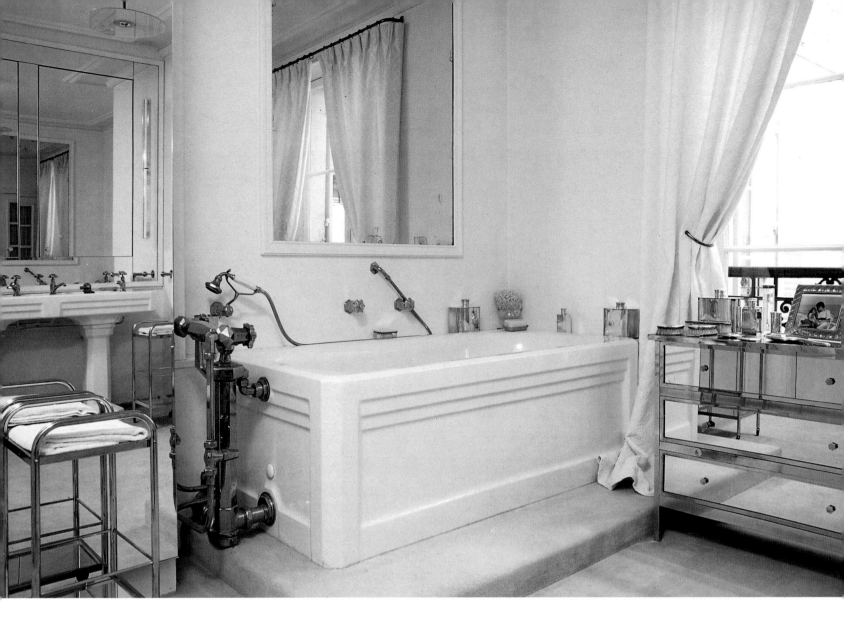

Pristine white, sparkling silver, and shiny mirrors at the Paris home of Luigi D'Urso and Ines de la Fressange reflect a natural flair for functional elegance, above. Free-standing porcelain washbasins, left.

In the Hamptons, Murielle Brandolini adds

a magic touch to a perfect country bath.

*Andrée Putman combines function, sim-
plicity, and elegance in the Paris home of
Didier Grumbach.*

Skylight and windows give a feeling of openness, enabling natural light to illuminate the room, above.

Marble tub and glass shower are set in an intimate sun-drenched bathroom perched on a Malibu cliff looking out on the Pacific Ocean, left.

With a dramatic use of glass walls and natural light, restrained elegance and unbridled nature are brought together in the California poolhouse of Barry Diller, right.

*A magnificent engraved antique bath completes the silver collection at
the Roman home of Dr. Giordano Restelli.*

In Paris, a turn-of-the-century bathroom has been restored to perfection
by architect Masakasu Bokura, above. Mr. and Mrs. Bokura's washbasin, right, was designed by glass-crafter Guillaume Saalburg.

At Calvin and Kelly Klein's beach house, a white porcelain antique tub standing on silver eagle's-claw feet captures impeccable American style, above. Classic white porcelain free-standing washbasin, left. Antique hand shower, right.

In South Carolina, at "All Brass" horse ranch, designed in 1933 by
Frank Lloyd Wright and restored to its original beauty by Joel Silver. The
intricate hexagonal designs inspire a sense of harmony and order, left.
A massive copper head fits the hexagonal wooden shower, above left.
The dressing area is in the style of a mountain lodge, above right.

In a Bel Air villa, Lisa Eisner captures the spirit of American style,
fitting the family-size bathroom with sea-green and sand-colored ceramic
tiles that create a distinctive California look.

In a Soho loft , white ceramic washbasins and an antique enamel tub reflect the free-spirited style of a New York artist, above.

A horse farm in Bridgehampton offers an exceptional setting for a country bath, right. Photo by Loic Raout.

The classic marble steam room at the exclusive Gentleman's Bath and Racquet Club, next to Claridges in London.

At the Royalton in New York, Philippe Starck created this streamlined bathroom for the penthouse suite. The bathroom features a custom round tub built into a concave wall, above. Two triangular Italian cut-glass vanities with stainless-steel sinks, left.

Andrée Putman designed a unique environment for a bathroom suite at Morgans, in the Murray Hill section of New York City.

Master bedroom in a Bel Air suite, California, above.

Turn-of-the-century bath at the Royal Monceau thermal bath and spa,
Paris, right.

At Claridges, in London: Nineteen-twenties original bathroom, left. *Nineteen-thirties marble-and-mosaic bath,* top right. *Nineteen-forties bathroom suite,* bottom right.

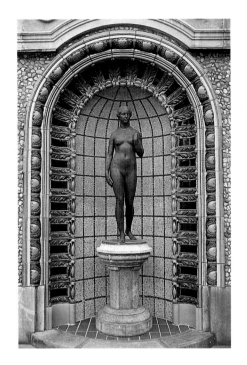

Thermal and Public Baths

CHAPTER THREE

The high art of bathing, as both a social and a cultural activity among Romans, declined along with their great empire. But even as life-styles and morality changed over the centuries, the earth's natural springs continued to attract an endless stream of bathers seeking to cleanse both body and spirit.

Many of the Roman bathhouses across Europe were trampled during barbarian invasions and left in

dust. But in the Middle Ages, convents and churches were built around the natural springs of those sites, thus preserving some bastions of cleanliness during that era.

Bathing is crucial to many religions, among them Islam. Suleiman the Magnificent, during the Golden Age of the Ottoman Empire in the sixteenth century, enlisted the architect Sinan to construct numerous mosque complexes in Turkey. The Koran dictates that without bodily cleanliness, prayer is "of no value in the eyes of God." Thus a hummum, a public place where the worshiper could bathe before prayer began, was typically erected near a mosque.

Dolamabahce Palace, Hummum (Turkish bath) of the Sultan, right. Entrance to the main bath, left. From the collection of M. Ali Tayar. Photos by Ozan Gulek.

In design, hummums preserved the basic shape of the Roman bath while dispensing with forums for any such diversions as exercise or intellectual pursuits. Grooming and massage were the order, along with nourishment. Islamic religion prescribes eleven conditions when a bath is required, among them the preparation of the bride for "purification" on the eve of her wedding. The sexes were strictly segregated: a man entering the women's quarters could be sentenced to death.

The hummums were popular through the 1920s, open to the public and free of charge. Many were built in Istanbul, home to the most elaborate of the structures; and some still operate today. The Turkish bath offers an exotic experience. The bathers enter a salon with a central fountain, where they lounge and smoke before being led to the bath by an attendant, the tellah. They are brought then to a slightly warmer chamber to disrobe and don a towel. The bath itself takes place in a third chamber, the hararet, or hot room,

thick with steam and so hot that special wooden shoes, called patten, must be worn to keep the feet several inches from the scalding marble. After this waterless bath, one experiences a rather excruciating massage, followed by a more soothing rubdown. The bather is finally scrubbed with scented soaps, rinsed, and led to a cooling area to rest and take refreshment.

The baths of Europe may well have been rescued from permanent obscurity when in France King Henry IV took a strong interest in the health and well-being of his people. Many of France's bath sites had fallen below standard as poor supervision allowed the waters to decline from their pristine natural state. The king designated his personal doctor to supervise the mineral sources, thermal baths, and fountains of the kingdom.

In 1633, King Louis XIII initiated a cultural phenomenon when, with his entire court in tow, he visited the mineral station of Forge-les-Eaux. This visit heralded the rebirth of the bath as

Topkapi Palace, Hummum (Turkish bath) of the Sultan, washbasin detail in the main bath, above. Main bath, right. From the collection of M. Ali Tayar. Photos by Ozan Gulek.

Jean-Léon Gérôme, The Bath, *c. 1880–*
1885. M.H. de Young Memorial Museum,
San Francisco, CA.
Hummum (Turkish bath) of Haseki
Hurren, main bath, left. From the collection
of Erol Cetin.

entertainment for the wealthy, an obsession that drew royalty, nobility, and bourgeois celebrities across great distances at great expense.

The baths attracted the likes of Montaigne, who basked in the waters of Plombières, Baden, and Lucques in search of relief from stones, inspiring numerous passages in his celebrated *Journal du Voyage en Italie.* The daughters of King Louis XV, Adelaide and Victoire, visited Plombières and

Vichy, while Madame de Montespan frequented Bourbon L'Archambault. Madame de Sévigné, the celebrated author, described Vichy in a letter to her daughter: "We mingle," she wrote, "we come and go, we take walks, we listen to mass, we bathe and drink the waters." While Napoleon Bonaparte challenged the world, his family kept itself busy by bathing and relaxing in the finest spas. At Aix-les-Bains, Napoleon's sister Pauline lost a fortune at the casino (Napoleon had authorized gambling at bath resorts in 1806), and Josephine once caused a commotion at Lake Bourset by almost drowning. Napoleon III was more leisure-minded than his namesake, often conducting not only diplomatic affairs but romantic interludes at Plombières, St. Sauvau, and Vichy.

By the turn of the century, the popularity of these chic spas had transformed many baths into virtual palaces: full-scale resorts, with lavish buildings and decor, superb service, and elaborate entertainment. After unwinding in the waters, guests could enjoy delicious gourmet meals and scenic strolls. They paraded among the idyllic gardens along the edge of the lakes observing and mingling, modeling the latest hairdos and clothes, enjoying an exotic mix of fashion, architecture, therapy, and intrigue.

Since that time, going to a spa has always been synonymous with luxury. Many modern spas have traded indulgence for a pristine, even Zen, approach to better health. The greatest extravagance of many spas may be their cost; but it is still possible to find thermal and mineral springs where one can absorb the benefits of the waters, along with a unique taste of spa culture, at a more moderate price.

Today, Budapest is the preeminent city of spas. Dozens lie throughout the city. The waters here have an excellent reputation for therapeutic value, combining as they do a high temperature with a high level of dissolved minerals. Soaking programs lasting three to four weeks are recommended for ailments ranging

from locomotor disorders to intestinal and cardiac troubles. Of course, a doctor's supervision is strongly suggested.

The baths of Budapest are delightfully atmospheric. One soaks in medicinal waters surrounded by Old World architecture. Thousands visit the baths each day, for both society and therapy. Among the most popular are Gellert, Szechenyi, and Kiraly. The Gellert Medicinal Bath is situated on the right bank of the Danube River: as early as the thirteenth century a hospital occupied the site. Noted for its fine therapeutic mud, the bath offers an open-air swimming pool with

Kiraly Public Bath, Budapest: exterior view, above. *The Turkish domed hall and thermal pool,* right.

Marble statue in the main entrance hall at Gellert Medicinal Bath, above.

Gellert's indoor swimming pool, whose water sparkles with bubbles of carbon dioxide, Budapest, left.

artificial waves, as well as a naturally carbonated indoor bath. Szechenyi is popular among those seeking especially hot waters. Its indoor and outdoor pools are busy even in winter. The rubber-coated chessboards in the baths provide a favorite setting for lengthy games. And Kiraly is an ideal choice for those seeking a taste of Turkish architecture; it was built during the 150 years of Turkish rule.

Situated between two volcanic belts, Japan offers countless natural thermal baths, furos. The tradition of public bathing dates back at least to A.D. 552 and to the dawn of Buddhism, which taught that such hygiene not only purified the body of sin but also brought luck.

Before entering the furo, one must endure a lengthy scrubbing ritual conducted on a wooden bench with a brush and a bucket. The bather then soaks in very hot water in an upright, seated position immersed to the shoulders. The experience of the Japanese furo embraces many of the senses. Fragrant woods are used

Gellert Medicinal Bath, Budapest: the men's shower hall, above. The men's thermal pool, with its large vaulted ceiling, is set in a splendid oriental decor, right.

to construct the tubs, and Zen garden compositions offer bathers a serene subject for contemplation as they absorb the water's heat.

In the frigid climates of northern Europe heat is a primary bathing component. The centerpiece of Finland's long bathing tradition is the sauna, some two thousand years old. Here is where folk-medicinal healing treatments were administered, where women bore their children and nursed them in the early weeks, and where the dead were prepared for burial. It is still a rather sanctified place, with sauna etiquette demanding silence and respect. Mixed company may bathe together only within the family circle: the family sauna is still a central part of daily life.

The first examples of saunas were simple pits dug into the earth, with heated stones to generate the dry, hot atmosphere. Hot stones remain the hallmark of the sauna, radiating warmth into a small surrounding room, which today is typically built of wood. Dousing the stones with water creates a vapor called *loyly* by the Finns. Body brushes, called *vihta* or *vahta*, and birch branches, are used to stimulate the skin and a healthy sweat.

Europeans arriving in America found a bathing tradition al-

ready in place. Native Americans and pioneers set aside their conflicts to share the waters of Hot Springs, Arkansas, one of the great spas of the United States. The first Europeans to discover the springs were the Spanish in 1541, and the site was later acquired by the United States from the French. Once Thomas Jefferson became aware of this natural wonder, the springs were given special attention and in 1832 became the first national reserve in the United States. Hot Springs became an immensely popular resort destination, peaking in

the early twentieth century, when elaborate and enormous bathhouses were erected. Only one survives today, though the springs, several luxurious hotels, and a museum remain.

Europeans need not cross the Atlantic in search of spas. In France, Evian and Vichy provide fine examples of the European response to the growing demand for spas. Vichy's enduring popularity inspired the construction of palaces, casinos, and opera houses in its vicinity. Today, the new buildings are tamer, emphasizing health rather than opu-

Surrounded by natural beauty, the outdoor thermal pool is open year-round at Szechenyi Therapeutic Bath, Budapest, above. The men's hall and thermal bath, right.

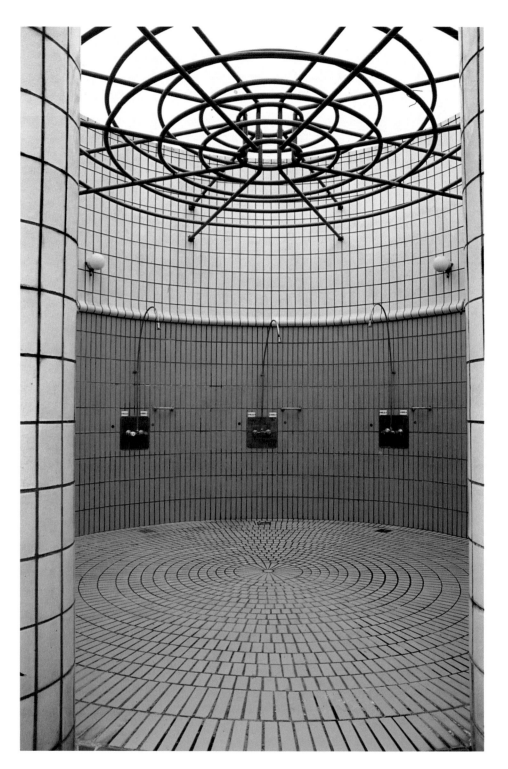

The outdoor communal shower at Gellert Medicinal Bath, Budapest.

Private treatment room and bath at Szechenyi Therapeutic Bath, Budapest, left.

lence. Vichy now has a vast new thermal establishment, with waters said to be beneficial for digestive troubles. Mud baths here are frequently used as a treatment for rheumatism.

Other noteworthy spas lie across the European countryside, from Montecatini and Salsomaggiore in Italy, to Baden-Baden in Germany and Bath in England. Many are the original natural-spring bathing sites that have been popular for centuries. While the scale of bathhouse architecture diminished, the popularity of bathing has endured.

Releasing their flow of fresh water for centuries at the same sites, the natural springs of Europe provided the setting for many pursuits: the search for God, for good health, for pleasure, prestige, and relaxation. The history of civilization flows through the waters of these baths: to linger in any of them today is to wade in waters much deeper than one might have imagined.

Private treatment room and bath at Terme Berziere, above. Photo by Ivan Terestchenko.

The central hall of Terme Berziere at Salso-maggiore, Italy, left. Photo by Ivan Terestchenko.

Natural hot spring at Takagarawa, Japan, above. Photo by Erica Lennard.

Like a Japanese princely retreat, the Golden Door Spa is set in an oriental garden, California, left.

A cedar-lined Finnish sauna in Connecticut, above.

Looking like an oasis, a Jacuzzi has been set in the natural environment of
a Malibu hill, right.

Bathroom Suites

*I*n French, the word for bathroom is *salle de bain. Salon de bain* might be a more apt description of the contemporary bathroom, which has evolved into a full-scale salon replete with all the accoutrements of a well-appointed suite.

In the eighteenth century, only the nobility had separate rooms reserved for bathing, and these they used infrequently, if at all. For the rest of the population, on those rare occasions when they bathed, a

Classical-style bathroom of artist Joachim Molina in Punta del Este, Uruguay. Photo by Cynthia Oliviera Cezar.

portable tub, often on wheels, was rolled into a room normally used for some other purpose.

Now, we relish the opportunity to bring other rooms of the house into the bathroom. No longer separated from the house, the bathroom is an integral part of the house. Contemporary bathrooms are marvels of design and decor. They may echo the home's design theme with overstuffed upholstered furniture and intricate mosaics or marble mantelpieces. They may evoke the feeling of a masculine library, book-lined and wood-paneled, or of an ultrafeminine boudoir, with lace window curtains, a mirrored dressing table, and floral wallpaper complemented by oriental vases filled with roses. If bathing in the living room was a necessity, and bathing in privacy was a luxury, then cleansing oneself privately in a bathroom that resembles an elegant living room may be the height of indulgence.

In the early days of Persia, there existed large and lavish bathrooms, where kings had vast, ornately decorated bath-

Monolithic marble tub at the home of artist Joachim Molina in Punta del Este, Uruguay. Photo by Cynthia Oliviera Cezar.

room suites. At Versailles, in the seventeenth century, Louis XIV had ornate gold-encrusted fixtures and expensive mirrors lining the walls of his seldom-used bathing chamber. Later, Napoleon, who bathed daily, uncharacteristically for his time, created a bathroom of such size and splendor that it was more like a ballroom. In the late nineteenth century, La Paiva, the infamous marquise who brought both glamour and scandal to Paris society, also brought exoticism to the Parisian bathroom. With onyx- and ceramic-lined walls, turquoise faucets, and a third spout that some think ran with champagne, she transformed a room in her home on the Champs Élysées into an opulent Moorish-style bath.

In the arts, sumptuous bathrooms appear more and more frequently as we approach the twentieth century. Edgar Degas's paintings of women at their *toilette* are renowned the world over. Sometimes his subjects are in simple surroundings, sometimes they are aided by servants, but

In a New York apartment, R. Brooke Ltd. combined mahogany, brass, and marble in a bedroom-size space to create a library-like bathroom with strong masculine architecture, fusing twentieth-century comfort with an Edwardian sensibility. Brass-grilled cabinets enclose books, towels, and bath supplies, above. The washbasin has been set in an alcove reminiscent of the Regency style, left.

always, these works are suffused by the sense of luxury and languor of the women and the cleansing rituals they perform. Pablo Picasso and Pierre Bonnard also painted women at their bath, documenting these intimate and graceful ceremonies for posterity.

Literature also gives us insights into the evolution of the bath. Balzac, in *The Physiology of Marriage*, reveals that private baths were becoming an expected privilege of the wealthy: "Your fortune, no doubt, gives your wife the right to insist upon a [private] bath," he wrote. In *La Curée*, Émile Zola described the magnificent pink marble bathroom of Mme. Saccard, complete with a chaise longue, and a glass-doored armoire. "The wonder of the apartment," wrote Zola, "the room about which all Paris speaks, is the bathroom." The fictional bath Zola created was shocking because it represented the beautiful heroine's extravagant expenditures and deliciously debauched life-style.

Courtesans, real and imagined, created luxurious baths that

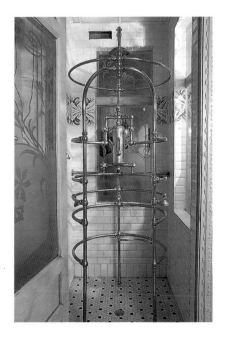

In Howard Kaplan's Manhattan home, the ample bath quarters are an extension of the living room.

Facing page: turn-of-the-century free-standing washbasin, top. *An antique shower from England,* bottom left. *Old-fashioned water closet with etched-glass panels and antique French telephone,* bottom right.

set the standard for style. Their special role in society gave them an enviable ability to live lavishly and celebrate their feminine wiles with scandalously elegant bathrooms that were a testament to their good taste and substantial fortunes. In the world of these beautiful, liberated women, the bathroom was a beguiling setting in which they could bestow their powers of seduction upon a select few.

Lavish private bathrooms became more common at the turn of the century when Elsie de Wolfe, whom some credit as the inventor of interior design, installed a bathroom larger than her bedroom at Villa Trianon. The room was decorated with consummate de Wolfe grace, a minimum of fuss, and a maximum of style. Filled with elegant furniture previously found only in the most refined living rooms, and boasting a large ever-burning fireplace, de Wolfe's creation forever changed the way decorators saw bathrooms.

Today, the desire to create elaborate bathrooms can turn this

room into the jewel of the house. No expense is too great, no decor too lavish, and no space too abundant to accommodate our daily ablutions. In California, size is tantamount to luxury. Entire floors are sometimes devoted to the bath. In New York or London, bedrooms are often sacrificed to create large, sumptuous bathrooms.

Not only has space expanded, but so has decor. The basic trilogy of tub, sink, and toilet has been elevated to high design. These functional fixtures are in harmony with the overall look of the room. Tubs are sunken and fitted with ornate, sculptural handles and spouts. Basins are inlaid with semiprecious stones, and toilets are so integrated into the design and decor of the room that they all but disappear. Classical shapes soothe the senses, streamlined designs promote calm at the end of a complicated day, and fireplaces add warmth and an elegant decorative detail. Even a simple window can add a touch of luxury to the bathroom, suffusing the room with light

Mysteriously, the bath at the Hotel Paiva in Paris, has three taps — it is believed that champagne flowed out of one, above. The oriental-style bath is richly decorated with inlaid onyx, marble, and turquoise ceramic tiles, left. Photo by Ivan Terestchenko.

while affording the bather a view of an English country garden, the canals of Venice, or the Manhattan skyline.

Architects and designers go to great lengths to re-create period designs. The range of choices is seemingly endless, and the availability of materials allows bathers to create the rooms of their dreams and lose themselves in fantasy.

A bathroom reminiscent of a Victorian novel could include authentic brass fixtures from England and a footed cast-iron tub. Another room might have vaulted ceilings, lush velvet drapes, and marble busts to create the feel of a Renaissance pavilion. A Japanese temple might inspire a designer to create a bathroom where tatamis and jade figurines lend to the cleansing ritual a Zen-like calm. Reverence for the opulence of the past could be the inspiration behind an ornate *salle de bain* of neoclassical design, where cleansing oneself in a marble tub fitted with gold faucets takes on an eighteenth-century flavor.

The bathroom suite is also a

In Milan, Romana Fabris used her distinctive style to combine art and function, left. The porcelain tub is encased in wooden panels, above.

highly functional setting. Period designs are often united with state-of-the-art technology to create body-conscious salons that conveniently combine exercise equipment with indoor hot tubs, steam baths, and multiheaded showers, additions that turn the bathroom into a private spa.

Whether it be for complete privacy, shared intimacy, or pure luxury, bathrooms allow for the creation of the ideal space. Exceedingly large, or comfortably spacious, these rooms permit us to express our personalities, indulge our fantasies, and relax in the splendor of a space created exactly as we wish.

In a Beverly Hills home, a limestone bathtub is flooded with sunlight, capturing true California style with a maximum use of light and space, top left. A mirror opens the room, bottom left. Bath and dressing area, above.

In Bel Air, California, Sandy Gallin chose plush carpeting and an extra-large sofa to create a generously proportioned living room and bathroom setting, left. The dressing area, above.

The magnificent antique copper tub brings the charm of the Old World into the Connecticut country home of Howard Kaplan, right. English antique porcelain washbasin decorated with blue chrysanthemums, left, above.

In a New York apartment, Alan Wanzenberg and Jed Johnson brought a second life to this former dining room. With the assistance of Alex Antonelli, a new bath space was created. The tub brought from Paris is porcelain-lined; the floor surface is a simple "Bottocino Classico" marble and "Kirkstone" inlay pattern.

In a Paris residence, inspired by a poem by Vincent van Gogh, a rare double bathtub has been set in sparkling white and deep blue ceramic tiles. "The Owl Standing by the Tree" is a clothes-rack sculpture by Alberto Giacometti. Vanity and dressing area, above.

In a Beverly Hills villa, the alluring style of a "well-dressed room" has been set by Rose Tarlow for a discriminating art collector, right. An exquisite lamp by E. Gallé gives a soft light to the tub area, above.

*In the South of France, an eclectic bathroom accented by architect
Ettore Sottsas' original style reflects the free spirit of businessman
Johnny Pigozzi.*

*In her Connecticut farmhouse, Diane Von Furstenberg transformed a
barn into a spacious spa.*

At her ranch nestled in a California canyon, Lynda Guber created a natural environment for her bath. Amethysts and crystals have been carefully set in the stones to attract positive energy.

Ronald Bricke designed this perfect his-and-hers bath for a Manhattan apartment. The oval lady's bathroom with fluted pilasters, domed ceiling, and inlaid Valencia marble flooring is connected to the man's study and bath by a shared shower corridor. Architecture by Robert A.M. Stern.

With a passion for perfection, Lynda Guber captures the art of Japanese bathing. The warm cherrywood tub is set in a solid slab of cool granite. Malibu, California.

In the Luberon, at Mrs. Cecille Chancelle's "Bastide," antiquarian
Nicole Altero transformed an old family room into an elegant traditional
salon de bain, left. In a decor capturing the spirit of Provence, an old-
fashion porcelain washbasin stands next to an antique fireplace, top.

In a Manhattan penthouse, Michael La Rocca placed the marble bathtub in the center of the room, right. He designed an adjoining exercise room, left.

In London, Isabelle Goldsmith chose Bennison fabric to bring warmth and elegance to a room reminiscent of the Victorian era, left. The shower and dressing area, above.

PHOTO BY DAVID SEIDNER.

Bathing

CHAPTER FIVE

*I*n the *Metamorphoses*, Ovid tells the story of how beautiful Diana, goddess of the hunt, turned the Actaeon into a stag when the unfortunate hunter saw the goddess at her bath. The myth about a beautiful strong woman surprised in an intimate moment has been represented throughout the ages in painting, sculpture, and literature.

Beauty and the bath has remained a common theme in the contemporary arts as well. Who can forget stunning Elizabeth Taylor in *Suddenly Last Summer*, emerging from the sea in a translucent white bathing suit, or Marisa Berenson bathing by candlelight in Stanley Kubrick's *Barry Lyndon.* Doris Day and Rock Hudson flirted and soaked connected by telephone in *Pillow Talk.* In Federico Fellini's *La Dolce Vita*, the beautiful Anita Ekberg defies convention and shocks all Rome when she bathes in the Trevi fountain.

Bathing is most often a private act, a solitary moment when we shed our clothes and indulge all of our senses. Throughout history, the bath has involved more than simply soap and water. The ancient Romans used aromatic oils before, during, and after bathing. Cleopatra's baths are famous for their opulence. In times when bathing was not popular, fragrant powders, creams, and perfumes were used to cleanse and scent the skin.

Every day, we need to cleanse our bodies, refresh our spirits, and replenish our energy. What better way to do it than with a bath supplemented by fresh

herbs and essential oils? Using ancient texts, literary allusions, and some old-fashioned trial and error, I have devised five simple recipes to turn the bath into a complete sensory experience.

At my farm in Connecticut we are surrounded with almost everything necessary to turn an ordinary bath into an extraordinary affair. Rose petals gathered early in the morning, before the dew has dampened their aroma, provide a luxurious, colorful fragrance for the bath. From the

Antique perfume bottles, above. *Diane Von Furstenberg's bathroom at her Connecticut farm,* right.

herb garden, rosemary, lavender, and other aromatic herbs can be used to infuse the bathwater with a burst of rejuvenating scent.

Whether or not you have your own garden, you can create some wonderful natural bath recipes with ingredients found at the local greengrocer, specialty food shop, or health and beauty store.

To make an herbal bath bag, place about one handful of herbs into an unbleached cotton or linen bag, or if you do not have one, in a fine handkerchief or a cheesecloth. Close the bag or tie up the four corners. Let it soak in the hot water. The herbs will release their color, energy, and fragrance. You can rub it gently on your skin, squeezing the bag like a sponge.

A few drops of essential oil in your bath along with the herbal bath bag can leave you feeling rejuvenated or completely relaxed. While you indulge your senses with wonderful scents, the essential oils will strengthen your vital energies and mobilize the body's own healing powers. Essential oils are extracted from an

enormous variety of aromatic plants, flowers, fruits, herbs, roots, seeds, and fragrant trees. Pure essential oils can be very expensive because the distillation process requires a tremendous amount of plant material to produce a small amount of pure oil. For instance one thousand pounds of jasmine flowers are needed to extract one pound of oil. Since some essential oils are extremely potent, they should never be administered internally. Never apply essential oils directly on the skin.

To make the bath a more beneficial experience you can refresh the air by putting a few drops of essential oil into a ceramic burner especially made to release the aroma of the plant essence throughout the air. The room will be filled with the energy and the scent of the aromatic extract.

Bathing is also about touch, the feel of the water against your skin,

the soap slipping over your body. Keep the bathwater comfortably hot, not scalding! Remember, a hot bath feels wonderful, but may weaken you temporarily. When you leave the bath, use a bath mat to keep from slipping and to protect your feet from a cold tile floor. After bathing, pamper yourself with plush towels and scented powders and creams before wrapping up in a thick terry-cloth robe or a smooth silk peignoir. Enjoy a cup of herbal tea.

Be sensible in the bathroom. It may be an old wives' tale, but bathing too soon after eating probably isn't wise. Take a bath before dinner or wait until you have fully digested your meal. Your body will feel better and your bath will be more enjoyable. If your doctor recommends showers rather than baths for you, please heed his or her advice. Most of these ideas for bathing and many of the recipes can be

adapted for use in the shower.

The bath is one of the few places where you can be totally alone and completely self-indulgent. You can easily create a bathing experience as elegant and beautiful as you wish. Dim the lights, light a candle, turn the music on low. Your bath awaits. Remove your clothes, luxuriate in your body, indulge your senses, and free your mind. Bath time is your time. Make the most out of this exceptional moment in your private spa.

Each recipe consists of three easy steps:

Step one. Put a few drops of essential oil into the ceramic oil burner.

Step two. Fill the bath bag with the herbs and let it soak under the hot running water.

Step three. Add the essential oils to the water and stir the bath.

A bath at the Hotel Paiva in Paris, left.
Photo by Ivan Terestchenko.

147

Amaury Duval, The Birth of Venus.

In the bathroom of Queen Maria Sofia at the Palace of Caserta, the massive bathtub is ornamented by a pair of lion's heads. The splendid vanity is carved in white marble, far right.

Contemplation

Let your body relax into this warm fragrant bath. Feel the soothing effect of the pungent roots of vetiver. Let the sweet and penetrating scent of wood entrance your spirit. Close your eyes, and indulge yourself in this quiet moment of contemplation.

BATH INGREDIENTS

5 drops sandalwood essential oil   *tablespoon of honey*

3 drops vetiver essential oil   *handful of lavender flowers*

Dissolve the oils in the tablespoon of honey and stir into the warm water. Submerge under the water the lavender flowers in the cotton bag.

AROMATIC ROOM REFRESHER

4 drops frankincense essential oil   *3 drops myrrh essential oil*

For the ancient civilizations of the world, frankincense and myrrh were as precious as gold. The Egyptians, Assyrians, Babylonians, Hebrews and Romans burned these gum resins in great quantities as an offering to the gods. The legendary Queen of Sheba crossed the Arabian desert with a caravan of aromats, frankincense, and myrrh to please King Solomon. In the New Testament they were offered by the three kings to celebrate the birth of Jesus.

At the Palace of Morvi, Gujarat, India: a sunken seashell marble tub,
right. Vanity and antique perfume bottles, above. Photos by Gwendoline
Ffoulke.

Enchantment

The rose is often called the Queen of Flowers. It has been a source of inspiration in Islamic poetry, and was cherished by the ancient Romans. It is said that when Cleopatra seduced Mark Anthony, she had the floor of her barge covered with a thick layer of rose petals. Today, red roses symbolize love and passion, white roses purity and tranquillity.

BATH INGREDIENTS

5 drops of rose essential oil   *handful of fragrant*
3 drops of essential oils of musk   *rose petals*
tablespoon of honey

Drop the oils into a tablespoon of liquid honey and hold it beneath the hot running water.

Scatter a handful of fragrant rose petals on the water. Enjoy this delightful bath.

AROMATIC ROOM REFRESHER

Four drops of rose essential oil and two drops of essential oil of sandalwood in the oil burner will add an oriental seductiveness to the atmosphere.

Renewal

To break away from a busy day, refresh your body in this fragrant citrus bath. It will leave you feeling rejuvenated and ready to enjoy a wonderful evening.

BATH INGREDIENTS

5 drops of essential oil of geranium
3 drops of essential oil of lemon
2 drops of essential oil of peppermint
juice of one lemon
handful of lemon grass in a cotton bag or cloth

Once the bath is drawn to a comfortable temperature, add the oils and the juice of a fresh lemon.

Squeeze the bath bag to release the refreshing citrus fragrance.

AROMATIC ROOM REFRESHER

Five drops of peppermint essential oil in the aromatic lamp will refresh and energize the room.

At the Palace of Caserta near Naples the magnificent late-eighteenth-century bath for Queen Maria Christina is set in a majestically decorated alcove. The finely sculptured white marble bath is lined in lustrous gold-plated silver. The taps are gilded brass, right. Sculptured cherubim over the door connecting the bath and the dressing area, above.

Exuberance

Jasmine flowers have been cultivated and gathered since ancient times in China and India, and more recently in the Mediterranean basin and in South America. Their strong sweet smell is intoxicating and acts as an aphrodisiac. The whiteness of their petals also evokes purity. Jasmine is the most expensive essential oil.

BATH INGREDIENTS

5 drops of jasmine essential oil

3 drops of ylang-ylang essential oil

2 drops of tonka bean essential oil

handful of orange blossoms in a cotton bag

Add the drops into the warm water and let the bathbag soak.

AROMATIC ROOM REFRESHER

5 drops of neroli essential oil.

In seventeenth-century Italy the Princess of Neroli had such a passion for orange blossoms that she even had her gloves scented with them. The scent became fashionable with the nobility, and soon the fragrant oil obtained from orange blossoms became known as neroli oil.

In a San Francisco room created by Diane Burn Evans, New York decorative art sculptor Bill Sullivan designed and hand-carved the painted wooden shell around a cast-iron tub, commissioned by Jessica McClintock, left. Photo Cookie Kinkead.

Amaury Duval, A Classical Bather.

Vitality

Rosemary and lavender grow on the hills beside the Mediterranean Sea, from Iberia to Sicily. Most of the fragrant purplish-blue flowers of the lavender are harvested on the high hills of Provence in the South of France. In ancient times both lavender and rosemary were greatly appreciated by the Greeks and Romans for the cleansing of body and spirit.

BATH INGREDIENTS

5 drops lavender essential oil
4 drops rosemary essential oil
3 drops orange blossom essential oil
tablespoon of virgin olive oil

handful of unbleached sea salt
handful of eucalyptus leaves
handful of mimosa flowers

Dissolve the essential oils in a tablespoonful of pure virgin olive oil and add to the bath water. Sprinkle the sea salt into the water. Put the eucalyptus leaves and the mimosa flowers into the cotton bag and let the combination diffuse its fragrant energy into the water.

AROMATIC ROOM REFRESHER

4 drops essential oil of cypress   *2 drops bergamot oil*

The aromatic scent of cypress and bergamot will uplift your spirit and make you dream of Provence.

In a Paris apartment François Catroux created a sumptuous neoclassical decor, right. The majestic washbasin is set in inlaid marble, below.

The natural bath at a Malibu house.

SOURCES

Where to obtain herbs and essential oils

Alfred Stevens, The Bather.

APHRODISIA

282 Bleecker St.

New York, N.Y. 10018

A selection of dried herbs, essential oils, and other bath and natural products.

KIEHLS PHARMACY

109 Third Ave.

New York, N.Y. 10029

Essential oils, baths, and cosmetics.

AROMA VERA

3384 South Robertson Place

Los Angeles, California 90034

LEYDET OILS

P.O. Box 2354

Fair Oaks, California 95628

AURACACIA

P.O. Box 399

Weaverville, California 96093

LOTUS FULFILLMENT SERVICES

33719 116th St.

Dept. AT

Twin Lakes, Wisconsin 53181

AROMATIC OIL COMPANY

12 Littlegate St.

Oxford, England

CULPEPER

21 Bruton St.

Berkeley, Sy.

London W1X7DA England

_ ADDITIONAL CAPTIONS _

Pages 8 and 9, Roman bath in Bath, England. Photo by IMG.

Page 10, C. Gleyre, *The Bath,* 1868. The Chrysler Museum, Norfolk, VA.

Page 13, Detail of the bath of Queen Maria Christina at Palace of Caserta, Italy.

Page 14, Jungle waterfall in Costa Rica. Photo by J. Carmichael, Jr., IMG.

Page 15, D. Ingres, *The Source,* 1856.

Page 32, Lucy Audouy created a gentleman's bathroom for her husband, Paul, that reflects a passion for nineteenth-century art.

Page 33, The Morning Bath.

Page 80, The open-air pool with artificial waves at Gellert Medicinal Bath, Budapest.

Page 81, Bronze statue in the alcove at the outdoor pool at the

Gellert Medicinal Bath.

Page 104, At the Palladian villa of artist Joachim Molina in Punta del Este, Uruguay. Photo by Cynthia Oliviera Cezar.

Page 105, Sealbert, *Woman Preparing Her Bath.*

Page 142, The statue of Diana in the Palace of Caserta, near Naples. Photo by David Seidner.